DISTINGUISHED LEAVES

Poems for tea-lovers

Quiller

DISTINGUISHED LEAVES

Poems for tea-lovers

Elizabeth Darcy Jones

FOREWORD BY

Nigel Havers

To my sister Wendy and Anna, Jackie, Julie, Logan,
Pat and Vanessa. What an amazing 'special blend'. Thank you.
You enrich my life with your presence.

Copyright © 2011 Elizabeth Darcy Jones
[For the sake of copyright Elizabeth Darcy Jones admits to writing these words,
but not without the assistance of numerous cups of leaf tea.]

First published in the UK in 2011
by Quiller, an imprint of Quiller Publishing Ltd

Designed by Andrew Barron

British Library Cataloguing-in-Publication Data
A catalogue record for this book
is available from the British Library

ISBN 978 1 84689 115 1

Printed in China

Quiller

An imprint of Quiller Publishing Ltd
Wykey House, Wykey, Shrewsbury SY4 1JA
Tel: 01939 261616 Fax: 01939 261606
E-mail: info@quillerbooks.com
Website: www.countrybooksdirect.com

CONTENTS

WARMING THE POT

Tea to the Fore!

Until recently, I wouldn't have relished being described as a tea...

I must confess that I have spent most of my life being a hardened coffee drinker mainly because I liked the look – the Italian Stallion at breakfast, Ray-Bans on, espresso in one hand, cigarette in the other.

I put up with the rather muddy bitterness, secure in the knowledge that it was 'cool', and tried to ignore the accelerated heartbeat that carried me through until lunchtime, when my hands stopped shaking.

However, now I have embarked on a new relationship with the delicate leaves and infinite variety of aromas that make up our national drink. I sup on 'builders' tea' first thing, to kick-start the day, followed by a cup of tasty Darjeeling for breakfast with a little milk. Nothing beats Lapsang Souchong at teatime, sometimes with a spoonful of honey if energy levels are flagging. After dinner I favour the palest Jasmine before retiring to bed and dreams of the Italian Stallion turning into an equally dashing thoroughbred!

I hope the contents of this exquisite and unusual little book will inspire you to put 'tea to the fore'.

NIGEL HAVERS

Before You Buy

A foamy sea of green in a simple black bowl, a paper thin porcelain cup cradling a lightly coloured but highly scented elixir, the taste of clay and sweet spices from a terracotta cup almost too hot to hold, or the sound of a spoon stirring milk and sugar in a cup painted with roses. Tea permeates different cultures like no other drink, and is equally at home in Japan, China, India or here in Britain.

Its ability to be prepared and drunk in so many different ways is one reason why tea is the world's favourite hot drink. Brewing loose leaf tea is easy and so much more rewarding than a tasteless tea bag. It is also the first step to discovering more about the remarkable people, places, processes, and plants that make the tea leaves in your pot.

Welcome to a wonderful world of flavour, culture and nature!

Tim D'Offay

Before You Pour

In my Retreat Dwelling tea is frequently and mindfully taken. The best cup is in the early morning, when with bleary eyes and muttering to myself I re-light the stove and put the kettle on. Candles are lit, offerings made and early morning meditation completed before I weigh out the tea leaves and add them to a warmed pot.

Ah… help is at hand!

Pausing at the open door I breathe in the pungent smells of wood smoke and damp earth, the night rain has ceased and among the dripping trees the birds are filling the air with sweet, tentative song. Pouring the boiled water onto the tea leaves releases another familiar fragrance. A few more precious brewing minutes and, cup in hand, I retire to my meditation cushion for the first sip of the day.

Dechi Palmo

Dechi Palmo is a Buddhist nun at Samye Ling Monastery and Tibetan Centre, Eskdalemuir, Scotland. She spends extended periods in retreat with only Tibetan sacred texts and tea for company.

As You Read

Poetry and tea are made for each other. Right now, both art forms are enjoying a quiet revival and increasingly being served up together. It's time to put the kettle on.

In the last eighteen months, I've been seduced by a handful of coloured leaves swirling round a pot. Paradoxically pleasing, I've discovered a drink that can simultaneously stimulate and calm, just like poetry. Still a novice when it comes to the world of tea, these poems chart the voyages of my taste-buds.

Refreshingly, tea and poetry are not online pleasures. You can't share a cup of tea through Facebook, nor does poetry resonate in quite the same way when read from a screen. Tea making and drinking, poetry writing and reading, engage all seven senses (add thinking and feeling to the usual five.) Yes, to me poetry demands tasting words and sniffing out meaning!

'Poetea' (poetry and tea) lends itself to individual and shared contemplation. At its best it reminds us of the intimate, accessible and unspoken aliveness that underlies this extra-ordinary thing called life.

Treat these poems as you would your tea leaves: let them steep. Allow the silence in between the lines to act as a strainer, filtering out yesterday's stories and tomorrow's 'to do list'.

Enjoy!

ELIZABETH DARCY JONES

茗

AUTHOR'S NOTE: As you can see, tea-making with loose leaf tea can be an artlessly simple business. A warmed pot, fresh water and time for the leaves to brew are the key essentials. Perhaps the only thing to add is that loose leaf tea has its particular preferences when it comes to how hot the water is! Very generally speaking, the less processed the tea (especially white and green) the cooler it likes its water. There's a wealth of advice on the subject – enough to fill a book – but most quality leaf teas will be accompanied with specific 'how to' instructions. And of course hundreds of tea-lovers are only too keen to offer you their preferred methods!

PS For those hesitating over a long menu of loose leaf teas for the first time, these poems provide a lead, a hint of character, but little more. Every tea is individual and all manner of things will affect the flavour – from the water to the attention of both maker and drinker. For the cost-conscious, don't forget that loose leaf tea is often cheaper than its bagged counterparts and the leaves of many teas can be used more than once, making them even more economical!

THE POEMS

All these poems concern one plant, *Camellia sinsensis*. The two varieties that we associate with tea are *Camellia sinensis sinensis* and *Camellia sinensis assamica*. From them, thousands of producing varieties have been cultivated.

These tea bushes produce leaves that differ depending on their 'terroir' and then acquire different characteristics through the way they're processed and blended. The types of tea we refer to form a glorious rainbow of 'colours' that I have used – loosely – to group the poems. This is not a straightforward matter, especially for a loose leaf tea virgin!

I leave it to the Tea Artisan and serious tea connoisseur to enjoy debating whether or not the following 'tea characters' occupy their rightful places.

In the meantime, rest assured that most teas seem to be endowed with some kind of health-promoting quality. The library of positive research based evidence confirming benefits to our well-being is growing. But however strong the health arguments may be, for me they come secondary to taste. Just let the leaves loose…

Fortune Favours the Tea!

Through the chink of the curtain of recessionary fears
Beneath the dirty blanket of economies and tears
There are people just like me and they're claiming that success
Lies in loving all the little things and knowing 'more is less'

And they're vital and they're free and they're loving poetry
And they're brewing up a steaming cup of Loose Leaf Tea!

Do you think that life is certain and the sum of all your years
Is best spent online surfing 'til your eyesight disappears?
Well, you've missed the revolution, but I'll tell you nonetheless
There's a crowd of potty strangers and they simply don't do stress

And it's plain for all to see that our radicals are free!
And we're brewing up a steaming cup of Loose Leaf Tea!

Now my ink must get a spurt on and start plotting isotheres
So the origins of tea will root deep down inside your ears
And the paradox is perfect we go back so we'll progress
We must grapple with geography, cast anchor from Sheerness

Are you vital? Are you free? Will you write a rhyme with me?
And are you up for brewing cups of steaming Loose Leaf Tea?

At a time when noted herbalist and Emperor Shen Nung
Was making myths in China, from a city like Nantung
Comes the tale that heating water for his early morning brew
Camellia leaves fell in the pot, Shen Nung thought, 'let them stew'!

And they're vital and they're free and they're making history
And they're brewing up a steaming cup of Loose Leaf Tea!

Well, I'm no history lover but before the reign of Sung
They named tea ch'a, it came in bricks and silk was called shantung
And scholars studied a classic work by the talented Lu Yu
Who some say chanted poetry – I'm not sure if that's true

He was quite a VIP, he had wisdom, he had chi
And I bet he brewed up steaming cups of Loose Leaf Tea!

Sublime Pu-erh was harvested and on the Emperor's tongue
It left its tang and people saw it calmed the highly-strung
Then fashion changed to powdered leaves (there's always something new)
The emerald of the younger tips has changed our story's hue!

And we're off and out to sea headed for tranquillity
Where they're brewing up a steaming cup of Loose Leaf Tea!

琼

Our journey's short, we disembark and find we're in Japan
Meet Eisai and his seeds (but he was no taipan)
He made his life a life of tea – and used his acumen –
To write the Kitcha-Yojoki[1] that's read by learned men

And he's vital and he's free and he knows just how to be
And he's brewing up a steaming cup of Loose Leaf Tea!

Tea Masters taught the Cha-no-yu[2] to the budding Artisan
While Geisha girls would sigh and sing and try to stay dead-pan
But the teahouse often doubled up as a rowdy gambling den
'til The Way of Tea (or chado) made it absolutely Zen

And from reading it we'll see that man's inner harmony
Comes from brewing up a steaming cup of Loose Leaf Tea!

We ought to take in culture from Kyoto to Hunan
But let's set sail for India in the sea-shoes of a man[3]
Who was generous and kind to many Chinese Gentlemen
And who also found the tea Camellia high in Fujian

Robert Fortune smuggled seedlings for a famous company
So we could brew up steaming cups of Loose Leaf Tea!

So the precious teas of China slowly moved towards the West
And in a hidden Cornish valley[4] they now find themselves a guest
But wherever tea is growing there'll be people just like me
Inspired by all the little things and writing poetry!

And we're vital and we're free and our creativity
Comes from brewing up a steaming cup of Loose Leaf Tea!

1 *The Kitcha-Yojoki or Book of Tea Sanitation by Eisai,*
   the first Japanese book on tea
2 *Chan-no-yu is the Japanese Tea Ceremony*
3 *Robert Fortune, who transported and planted over*
   twenty thousand tea seedlings for The East India Company
4 *Tregothnan, near Truro*

This is not intended to be a history of tea although it may whet your
appetite to discover more. John Weatherstone's Tea – A Journey in Time
is a visual and literary delight, and Jane Pettigrew has written many
excellent books.

WHITE

WHITE: the colour of purity. White tea is barely processed at all ('withered' and very gently dried) and is traditionally picked at daybreak. Only the tiny immature buds are used, their fine, downy white hairs giving the type its name. It's unsurprising, therefore, to learn that white tea is very delicate in flavour.

White tea is produced in just a few regions, principally in the four provinces of north east Fuijan in China and in Sri Lanka, and considered very rare. I couldn't drink it out of a mug! This is truly 'Zen tea'.

Bai Mu Dan

She welcomes death our virgin Bai[1] Mu Dan
Her coffin is a porcelain sedan
Her sigh is cool, she tastes of dappled light
She's so composed she doesn't need a fan

Bai Mu Dan's a girl who never quite
Grew up, an angel sheathed in white
She takes you gently to the heart of now
Where stillness reigns and you give up the fight

Bai Mu Dan kneels down, her silent bow
Extinguishes the what, the why, the how
Admire her drowning tips of peony
Honouring Advaita and the Tao.

1 *Also sometimes called Pai Mu Dan*

Snowbud

close your eyes and
feel hot snowflakes on your tongue
water from an elusive mountain stream
caught in cupped hands of a wistful child

this is a sexist tea (save for connoisseurs
embracing sensitivity)
for would-be virgins
anxious to meet that girl again
anxious to have their innocence
restored

fit for resurrection
Snowbud partners
Fauré's *In Paradisum*
sipped from the finest
Chinese blue so thin the moon
shines through
Snowbud's pale and chaste
murmur a prayer before you taste

White Silver Tip

I chose you as you're rare and dare to play
with words, while you inspect this jar
of fragile glass, and then baptise my day
so slowly I don't know that you're a star
until I brew a second time and here you are
eye-bright with taste and subtle smell of hay

the silver of the dawn is rising in my chest
allowing each new bud (unborn and sweet) –
that's picked before the sun moves west
before the pickers dare to stop and eat –
to purify my mind, my heart, my blood
so when I meet the day I'm at my best

GREEN

绿

GREEN: nature's canvas. Green Tea is still the tea most frequently drunk in Asia and the Far East. It is particularly associated with Japan, where the leaves are often powdered. But it was also the first tea to be drunk in Britain, as early as 1673, by Catherine of Braganza and her friend the Duchess of Lauderdale in their respective homes by the River Thames in South West London.

Producing Green Tea involves 'cooking' or 'steaming' young tea leaves to seal their colour and preserve their freshness.

I used to think that Green Tea was meant to be bitter, but at the time I was drinking bagged inferior stuff. What a revelation when I tasted the liquor from huge ribbons of green! Green Tea is not bitter but sweet (perhaps with the exception of Pinhead Gunpowder) and sends my senses straight into the undergrowth of heaven, my dad's allotment.

Authentic Dragon Well

This garden walled by winter box and stone
begs me write a sonnet but I'm shy
can I recall the pristine West Lake sky
while sitting here in Surrey all alone?
this tea has always been beyond compare
'though 'less is more' describes my Dragon Well
its leaves are grassy, gift a peachy smell
its liquor soft, like misty morning air
but that omits the tips, adroitly fired
by masters wearing sweat and soul-stained sleeves
sustained throughout the harvest by their pride
using tools their ancestors acquired
their marriage is to many thousand leaves
each and every one a virgin bride.

Genmaicha

Japanese girl
in New York is walking
her yellow dress
is talking

Japanese girl
is making popcorn
of my mind and
stops me thinking

Japanese girl
is reflected in the sunshine
of tea
I'm drinking

Japanese girl
across the pond
you bring the yellow
cabs to Richmond

Japanese girl
in New York
is Genmaicha
beguiling
and smiling

Jasmine Pearls

Lick your lips for Jasmine Pearls
curves and softness, hair that curls
and tempts your mouth to form an 'O'
through which her jasmine scent will flow

Jasmine travels round your mouth
before she takes your taste-buds south
and makes your senses gently glow
in places only you would know

velvet tea for Grown Up Girls
whose conversation slowly swirls
and turns into a nom de plume
for Jasmine's full and rich perfume.

绿

绿

Matcha Latte

Matcha must be made from Sencha Green
to taste like ground kimono, silky smooth
that settles on your lips, her milky sheen
smells of kisses – puts you in the groove

adjectives retreat afraid of cliché
but 'creamy' falls asleep on Matcha's chest
so apposite the poet lets it stay –
of all descriptions this suits Matcha best

Matcha's unimpressed by noise and drama
disappears before you realise
she's worked her milky magic, made you calmer
teased you with her inky almond eyes.

Moroccan Mint

Moroccan Mint Tea is refreshingly green –
A genie that hides in an old silver pot
It's potent but cooling, full bodied but clean
Its secret? The strength of its gunpowder shot.

Moroccan Mint Tea releases its potion
Of sweetness and youth into little glass vials
Its genie will serve you with utter devotion
His only reward your laughter and smiles

Moroccan Mint Tea has magical power!
Its viridian tips relieve and restore
Reputed to make creativity flower
Ideas will start flowing as you start to pour.

Pinhead Gunpowder

let bitter bang you up and bruise your tongue
the pinhead speaks to sinners, rusts its tin
and sacks the spoon, serves the thug
gratuitously greening unglazed skin

if twitter tanks you up this tea's for you
if you're friends with facebook – fill your cup!
this tea stalks sleep in snakeskin shoes
busts writer's block and online blues

crave coffee? pinhead's caffeine in a hot
wired crate, its pinnate leaves leach hate
it's wild, the child that mild and meek forgot
to tame, tattooing taste-buds with its name

Toasted Hojicha

Sit yourself on warm tatami
Guided by a silent man
Join this ancient ceremony
In a teahouse in Japan

Taste of autumn in its liquor
Tawny toasted Bancha Green
Draws itself – and you – the drinker
To a place that's in between

Hojicha then bows before you
As you stare at empty space
Leaves you with his smile of knowing
Mirrored in the tea bowl's face.

BLUE

BLUE: soothing, sad, the sea. Blue is fluid and difficult to pin down, like Oolong which – I should mention – is no longer usually termed 'blue'. Nevertheless, some Oolongs have a bluish tinge to the leaves while others are really a beautiful 'sea-green' and many are golden brown!

Oolong is more processed than Green Tea – it has begun to oxidise, but less so than Black Tea. What particularly distinguishes Oolong is that it's produced from tea bushes that have distinctive long leaves. The flavours, qualities and appearance that belong to Oolong are many and diverse.

These leaves can be subjected to all kinds of punishment to extract the full range of their myriad flavours: bruising, baking, tumbling, rolling, twisting and even curling.

Amber Oolong

He's a golden headed lad whose ruddy cheeks
Confirm he grew up living on a farm
He's somewhat shy, the friendship that he seeks
Is blanketed in clumsy boyish charm
You sense before you order that he speaks
In simple which, this once, will do no harm
And yet his warmth ignites forgotten embers –
Amber liquid that your heart remembers

One cup and you are his, your chi runs hot
You feel his passion rising in a rush
And all you knew you were but had forgot
Erupts! Admit it you've a teenage crush
On Amber Oolong! Peer into the pot
And hope that he'll ignore your second flush
Abandoning decorum, all your senses reeling
You colour and he looks up to the ceiling.

Formosa Oolong Top Fancy

Oolong Top Fancy's all Gok Wan! His blend
Of fashion-conscious flavour's right on trend
No stiffness in his lips, they're warm and soft
He's subtle, sweet and sensuous… he's your friend.

Dress him in a stylish shantung suit
Purse your lips as if you play the flute
And praise his colour when he bares his shirt
This flirt admits he's handsome, gold and cute.

He's full of tempting teasing Eastern charm
His mission is to take you in his palm
And breathe sweet nothings up your nose
Until his giggles ripple through your calm

Oolong Top Fancy's all Gok Wan! His blend
Of fashion-conscious flavour's right on trend
No stiffness in his lips, they're warm and soft
He's subtle, sweet and sensuous… he's our friend.

青

Dong Ding!

You wouldn't know she's daughter of the King
Of All, she makes His subjects sing
With green, she's young and coiled up in the jar
Not tight, but loose, the promise of the Spring

Dong Ding's the sister of that spiral girl
Pouchong, delighting in the different ways they swirl
As all their grassy sweetness is released
Dong Ding's the one with bounce within her curl

For introducing Oolong to a child
She helps to make that step past soft and mild
An easy hop to grown up, dear Dong Ding
Delivering a hint of something wild.

Miss Pouchong

Pouchong[1]? She dresses in Chanel
A classic suit, a pin in her lapel
Her scent is craved by gentlemen
And ladies love her just as well

Pouchong's demure – all hooks and clips
All ruffle, pout and primness on my lips
Demanding to be drowned not once but twice
Before her spirals hang with citrus drips

Determined we will brand her strong
She drowns again and sings a final song
So sweetly that we're tempted to agree
That 'though her suit is green she's pure
Oolong.

1 *Also known 'Baozhong', pronounced 'Bow-jong'.*
Personally, I think the sound 'poo-chong' suits her
fragrance and character 'just as well'.

Phoenix Honey Orchid

she's a perspicacious Oolong
named so she won't fit neatly in a poem
fit for drinking in four minutes precisely
she's particular
rustles her phoenix feathers
and speaks concisely
while her honey nips you with
not quite citrus quite contrary

what else can I say?
she's pert and precious
words like ashes skitter
rise in characters I can't translate
pleased she's a sky away –
always shies from description
tantalisingly out of reach
Phoenix Honey Orchid
with the smell of peach

BLACK

BLACK: When I discovered the Chinese name for Chinese Black Tea I saw red… because Black Tea is known as Red Tea (Hong Ch'a). I'm going to stick to calling it black, at least until I visit China.

Black tea is what we're likely to be most familiar with – fully oxidised. Machine-made (crush, tear and curl or 'CTC') Black Teas from India, Sri Lanka and – increasingly – Africa, make up most of the world tea market. And let's acknowledge the billions of satisfying machine-made cups of black tea brewed worldwide. However, in the last ten years or so Chinese Black whole leaf teas have come back into favour in Britain. There are some real treats to explore!

Black teas are the teas to which we can acceptably add milk, although some seem better suited to a slice of lemon.

If you want to reduce the caffeine, by the way, rinse the leaves first and you'll reduce it by up to fifty percent without losing any flavour.

Afternoon Tea from Cornwall

My gaze falls on the Fal – it's dead on three
Tregothnan's sun makes butter of my bones
Someone's thinking, 'Now's the time, it's time for tea!'

Tourists talk of Eden, Marazion and the sea
While clotted cream is spread on fresh baked scones
My gaze falls on the Fal – it's dead on three.

Torn leaves – from bushes only feet away – are free
To swell, and fill the pot until it groans
Is someone thinking, 'Now's the time, it's time for tea?'

It's young, organic, grown right here and, naturally,
It tastes of rivers steaming smoky tones
My gaze falls on the Fal – it's dead on three.

Best check your watch and travel West with me
Read the signs! Switch off your mobile phones!
Everybody's drinking. 'Now's the time, it's time for tea!'

I reconnect to that which no one owns
My gaze falls on the Fal – it's dead on three
This someone's thinking, 'Now it's time, the time for tea!'

Assam

Girls who love an all night raver
Scottish lassies prone to claver[1]
Wrap their fingers round a cup
Of Assam tea when they wake up

Muscle men will never waver
When you ask them for a favour
If you serve them Assam first –
Reminds them of their deeper thirst!

Women, wearing lives of labour
Like a tea with bags of flavour
Sure to stop them feeling down:
Assam is their choice of brown.

Gilbert O'Sullivan loves to savour
Assam (and his semi-quaver
Sings to lyrics in tea's praise)
Assam, Assam tea always!

1 *Scottish 'to gossip'*

Big Smoke

this smoke travels northwards
your stomach smells it
before its Big rests
in the small of your back

this smoke is steam
no City here
it's wood and peat and water talking –
a Scottish burn, Sri Lankan stream

this is pavement, patio tea
to be strained in a sieve
so its charcoal flecks
drive a swoop of sparrows
to the bottom of your cup
and prompt your gaze skywards
always rising up!

the lick of cinnamon
moves through your shoulder blades
until its sweetness fades and
all that's left
is the shadow of the sparrows
on your tongue
and the taste of warm

Brother Bohea

Lapsang's brother is a seer
his hair is long
he's up at dawn
to light a fire
it softly smokes
you get the idea…
of brother Bohea

Lapsang's brother is a seer
he's not strong
like Lapsang, born
to something higher
and his smell evokes
the name of Hosea…
but he is Bohea

Lapsang's brother is a seer
he is souchong
he is withdrawn
but wants to inspire
and his flavour strokes
away all your fear…
this is Bohea.

A Very British Darjeeling

Margaret Hope's Second Flush
Comes with a rush
All Anglo-Indian, Raj and Royal
Smells of wealth from the Empire's soil

Margaret Hope – according to rumour –
Had a great sense of humour
She's a tea that sings *Rule Britannia* with passion
Believes that good manners are always in fashion

I suspect Margaret Hope is the kind of Great Aunt
Who raises her cup and says, 'never say can't'
A companion who's rather appealing
Margaret Hope is a tea from Darjeeling.

紅

Earl Grey

He's such a Nigel Havers of a tea
His grey is warm and lustrous as a pearl
His scent reminds you you're nobility
He treats you like a lady not a girl

His breath of bergamot is from an age
Of Georgian fancies, lace and lemon curd
But you and not the tea take centre stage
Earl Grey is quiet – he does not say a word

This titled tea insists that we're polite
He puts a finger on our longing lips
And as he does he fills us with delight
We taste him taking tiny little sips…

Dreaming of his slender fingertips…

In Extremis Tea

it lives and gives of itself in the dread and hope-denuded place
its common currency
its only saving grace
is the flavour of strong sweet brown from plastic cups (too thin)
drunk in the dead of night while humming fluorescent strips (too bright)
numb your mind to the question 'who's the next of…'
intensify every presence in the absence of…
that's when with appalling ease
tea keeps us continuing

红

Keemun Rose

she's a warm rose that just dropped into China
she's lipstick and eyeliner
she suits a 'just us girls together' chat
she'll lift you when you're feeling flat
she'll make you purr like a Cheshire cat
she soothes you just like that

Lapsang Souchong

Lapsang stirs at four, he lights his smoky
cigarette that tastes of all things slow and
smells of damp dark woods where pandas go
he lets its earthy fragrance speak for him
he lets the taste of black that's lingering
snuff out the bright and crazy of the day
his brand of lazy is a world away
he takes you by the tongue
until you understand that you're among
the silent pines of China's Wuyi Mountain
and sense that night has come

Russian Caravan

this tea has tang

its caravan scent is
leather, sweat and mountain dust
that penetrates thick folds
of felted, belted
tight mistrust

this tea has tang

the cold war thaws in one stiff motion (cup to lip)
no common words but a synchronistic sip that prompts a sound
(half-sigh, half-gulp, half-ah!)
the breath that follows
mingles

this tea has tang enough to last

'til vodka thrusts its sword into narrowing eyes
the tea leaves
dregs die
peace grieves
talk returns to spies

this tea had tang

its caravan scent was
leather, sweat and mountain dust
its strong familiar brew
penetrated folds of felted, belted tight mistrust
for an hour or two

Vanilla Black

neither shiny nor jet
not inky though wet
but creamy
and steamy
this tea's in the groove for smoothing a frown

unlicensed to thrill
vanilla is chill
but warms you
informs you
its black is a deep shade of brown

not flaky and gloss
not Jonathan Ross
but soulful
a bowlful
will wrap you in comfort and s-l-o-w life down

红

Vanilla Mint

You are my Mr Darcy of a tea
all wet vanilla lawn pressed flat
against a smooth taut torso, China black

your name (so bland it doesn't give a hint
of what's beneath that frosty arrogance of mint)
makes you the perfect choice for me…

… understated masculinity.

Yellow, Red and Pu-Erh

黄
黑
洱

YELLOW, RED AND PU-ERH: As we reach the Autumn point of this collection, we meet its swirling colours – yellows, reds and the rich dense hues of Pu-Erh. Yellow, of course, also reminds us of Spring. Yes, this is rather a mixed bag with portly Pu-Erh sitting like royalty at the end.

Pu-Erh is a fermented post-oxidised tea and the best is even termed 'vintage', like a fine wine, port or champagne. It can be – as I call it – 'put to sleep' to age and mellow for months or years. Some people recommend washing it before drinking to 'awaken' it. It is still sometimes compressed into cakes or bricks, just as it was in ancient times to make transportation in caravans easier, the leaves chipped off to make tea when required.

Pu-Erh doesn't taste like tea as we know it, but its aftertaste seems to me to be deeply sustaining. You will either love it or hate it – just like a certain brown spread!

Huo Shan Mountain Buds

not quite green
not quite white
not so sharp
that it gives you a bite
almost yellow
not quite mellow
best served hot
best described
by what it's not

Red Lychee

polka dot retro in a beret
pick her and hear her shriek, 'Hooray!'
sweet as the kiss of pink gin
cleaner than Aggie's kitchen

China delivers her on time
she likes to dance to this rhyme
knows that you'll find her quirky
reassuringly perky

little Red Lychee's Made For You
find her in Rome and in Timbuktu
why can't we buy her at Waterloo?
bet that you can in Katmandu!

medicine when life is humdrum
sings from the tin that she's yum yum
she'll make you start serving high tea
all for the sake of Red Lychee

tea when you're on the school run
tea when you wanna have fun
tea when your really hot date
tells you he's gonna be late

little Red Lychee's Made For You
find her in Rome and in Timbuktu
why can't we buy her at Waterloo?
bet that you can in Katmandu!

Yunnan Red Cloud

you must be introduced to Master Liu
as I was, by surprise and yet on cue
he summons up that crazy word conundrum ––
his mastery of turning humdrum leaves to liquid light
defies his youthful skin
a battered photograph
seals in tight his beaming grin

I wonder if the Master Mr Liu
is smiling in his dreams
as Red Cloud silently disperses – what?
I can't divulge, except it was a knot
held in a bulge below my cheeks

these rusty leaves breathe
where tea and air and sense
were barred by tense negativity
but now red cloud is playing
with my chi
and the song of spirit
rolling up and down my spine
feels DIVINE!

my face is tingling
nostrils glow
'thank you Master Mr Liu'
in your dreams a foreign lady
sneezes
and smiles back at you

Emperor Pu-Erh 1996 and 1998

Remove your shoes before you drink Pu-Erh
Immerse yourself in Chinese lore and myth
Assume the posture of an Emperor
Imagine you're a holy hieroglyph
Revered by monks, who bathe before they stroke
Your stony surface, fingering the clear
Sharp lines that spell your name as if you spoke
Direct to each, extinguishing his fear
I see you hesitate to take this pose…
You want to wash Pu-Erh before you meet?
Pu-Erh is your reflection and he knows
Each speck of dust belongs there on your feet!
Remember that you dance your own duet
He's wide awake before you make him wet

Are you prepared? Now sit stone still and drink
You'll find your substance tastes like dense deep felt
Eradicating any need to think
You know that this is where you've always dwelt
Self-awareness percolates within
You see yourself as Queen or King or Tsar
Comparison would be a mortal sin
For now you know exactly what you are
But stop! The Emperor forbids you speak
He gags your mouth, ignores your monkey mind
And asks what validation would you seek?
Who cares if others judge you cruel or kind?
Pu-Erh reveals innate security
He cultivates your soul's maturity

黃
黑
泙

And as for years and valuing his age?
Like my own, I'd rather let you guess
No! No! Accept it's better not to gauge
Since Pu-Erh cake reflects our timelessness
Without forethought your forehead smoothes
Umami silences dis-ease, desire
With each infusion everything improves
There's nothing more to yearn for or acquire
And yet three sonnets down I can't describe
The fullness of this venerable tea
Like life you must experience – imbibe!
Pu-Erh's the taste of non-duality
The Emperor laughs – as if to say, 'Of course –
I am your own felt unity, your Source'

OTHER FRIENDS

Oddly enough, it's when we start trying to distinguish between scented teas, tisanes and herbal infusions that confusion descends. Which ones should we call teas? My tea teacher tells me that a tisane is a mixture of tea with something added, like rose petals or bergamot – which makes Earl Grey a tisane rather than a tea! This is not the case for scented teas apparently, when the tea-leaves have actually absorbed the scent of the flower or herb, as in Jasmine Pearls.

But are 'teas' that come from bushes or plants other than *Camellia sinensis* actually teas? I don't know, and I'm not sure it really matters. The common factor is that they are steeped in hot liquid, usually water, and that the leaves, chopped flowers or bark are not consumed. No doubt I shall learn the precise distinctions over time.

As for Lovers' Tea? Perhaps this blend is exempt from quality control. After all, it's infused with love!

Camomile

Camomile's a coward
weak and born a limpid
pool of quite insipid
tea that's prone to sleeping

Camomile is wispy
speaks in quiet lispy
tones, that dull and numb you
good to drink when weeping

Camomile is boring
tipple of the lazy
smiles to see you snoring
while her leaves are steeping

Irish Velvet

she's an Irish jig that's gone to sleep
she's a rubbed down Dublin filly after
the race is won she's the deal that'll
keep you humming for years to come

she's neither this nor that but
all you'd say to you if you were your own lover
and she's that blissful bumming around flavour
that no one else but you can savour
the moment when desire dissolves

she's a classy tart with a slug of Irish
comfort artlessly thrown in
she's the feel of flawless skin
she's the day drowning
in a night of sin

Lemon Verbena

The place is number twenty-two[1]
For poets it's The Place to be
And I'm assured they always do
            Verbena Tea

It smells like stuff called Keep-Away
Once used to keep your lawn cat free
But this tea keeps cold sores at bay!
            Verbena Tea

I must admit I love its smell
And while I'm writing poetry
It steeps, and steeping suits it well
            Verbena Tea

1 *The Poetry Café at The Poetry Society, London*

Lovers' Tea

it marks the end of steamy sex
of fluids exchanged and matted hair
your love is now a googolplex[1] –
          beyond compare!

you make the tea then quite forget
it's made and leave it standing there
in favour of that other wet
          you'd rather share

tea remade and back to bed
baptising this, your quilted lair
drinking from each other's cups
          'cos you're a pair

the blend is immaterial
you might as well be drinking air
you spill it on your cereal
          and just don't care

the pause that it insists you take
reminds you both to take things slow
you cannot hurry Lovers' Tea
          as lovers know

1 *The world's second largest number with a name.*

Wild Rooibos

Wild Rooibos is Herald Kanley Popgins
CHILLED

fallen scarlet cumulus scattered
LUMB

farmed by Dr Frikkie Strauss
home visits only - bedside TLC –
unwieldy schedules heading to diversion
VERY ZIGGY

dying for…

mouth merried squatness pooling
born free lion stretching
tongue trumpeted redpur dot spilt sssssspreading
bushes releasing vast clues HERE
promising post-coital curlup
unrigged derrness
hummed burring
flesh sighing

in Surrey scrubbed out sun too!
stealing Mr Bluesky
no boo
just bunked off stupor
descending
descending
down

TEA PEOPLE

It's a funny thing, but as I began to think of teas in terms of characters, I started seeing characters in terms of different teas!

My exploration has made me friends. I am privileged to be meeting 'tea people' who dedicate their lives to tea. Without exception every true tea-lover I've met has also been a life-lover, in awe of their fellow Tea Artisans and the history of which they are a part. None would call him or herself an expert, indeed, most Tea Artisans prefer to live without any kind of title.

But tea-lovers are not only those who work in the industry. If you're reading this book, I bet you're a tea person too. Watch out – I'm looking for candidates for the 'tea-people' section in the next volume!

Henrietta Lovell

I see her sitting prim she does not stir
So small and shy – a frozen pipistrelle
Sipping Great Aunt's tea is de rigueur
She does not know Darjeeling's cast its spell
Only the yellow sofa can foretell
What she's tasted is a force majeure!
The liquid fills the child's fontanelle
She understands that tea is her milieu

Her father's death blocks out the tinny whirr
Of weary leaf-less work but she can tell
Beneath her grief her future is a blur
And then, on Hong Kong air, she sniffs that smell
Instantly the view's no longer hell
The yellow sofa's heard her cri de coeur
The tea leaves circle like a villanelle¹!
She understands that tea is her milieu

Now Artisan and also connoisseur
Discreet about her famous clientele
Save one – a friend – and noted restaurateur
Who knows his terroir and his Dragon Well
She talks between her bites of his quenelle
Unaware that she's a raconteur –
A shining pearl that's safe within its shell –
We understand that tea is her milieu

Prince of Neptune! Bless this mademoiselle
The tea-leaf's bold agent provocateur
The yellow sofa loves you Ms Lovell
You understand that tea is your milieu

1   *Afternoon Tea in Cornwall is an example of a*
villanelle (see page 41)

Henrietta Lovell is a well-known figure in the tea
industry and a supplier of rare teas to some of London's
top restaurants and hotels. She is also on a mission to
'de-bag' Britain.

Jonathan Jones

A blend grown in the rich soil of history and plants might make
for a rambling man,
short on mystery and long on toiling,
slow to reach his boiling point…
we couldn't be more wrong!

Retake, rewind and I'll try to be concise!
This Tregothnan Treasure – like others in its store –
will not ignore the mysteries and synchronicities
that give life spice
that picked him up and potted him with a bunch of Camellia leaves
to steep for years, visiting Taiwan and places East,
observing, tasting, planting, letting his knowledge deepen,
feasting, carefully dissecting, collecting, protecting
his wealth in a mental Wardian Case[1] where plants and plans
miraculously found space to grow…

in Cornwall
at the home of the Boscawens where the Fal flows slow
along Tolverne to a place where nature tries her best
is sheltered from the wild west winds but not from Lady Falmouth
(looking stern)
here Jonathan Jones arrived, and grinned
his passion burned

and warmed Tregothnan where walls of Camellias rose up
unaided as if to promise their culinary counterparts success
perhaps by simply being there they part-persuaded the family
to maintain their fame, blame their eccentricity and
'let the man grow tea!'

ten years on Tregothnan's Treasure strides – a blond and
compact father of the land – who wears his pride for his bushes
in that humble way that only horticultural fellows truly understand
he credits his journey back through his ancestry
to childhood memories of strong sweet tea as he sips his own blend
         – 'Afternoon' –
explaining how so many opportune events and meetings led him
here

and now they're leading you and me
me writing
you reading
how Jonathan Jones learned from the snowy mountains in Japan
'Can I grow tea in Cornwall?'
'Yes you can!'

1 *The Wardian case was originally a sealed glass case designed to transport
young plants and seedlings, especially long distance. In particular,
Robert Fortune used Wardian cases to transplant over twenty thousand
tea plants from China to India for The East India Company.*

*Jonathan Jones is Garden Director at The Tregothnan Estate, in Cornwall –
home to the UK's only tea producing plantation.*

Pei Wang

His reputation saves me from the cold
The courtyard cobbles grapple with my feet
Propel me to his door (they read my tang)
I'm greeted by umami yet it's sweet:

this is Pei Wang!

I face two shining orbs obscured by glass
A subtle moon-smile no one could ignore
Lights up the room with promises of Spring
In quiet formality that's waiting for…

the tea to sing!

Pei's a paradox, he's young but old
He's Pu-Erh Big Snow Mountain Green
A giggle sits beneath complexity
He makes me feel as if I'm seventeen!

I love his chi!

I leave the teahouse feeling rather bold
Pei takes me by the arm, it starts to snow
I want to stroke the cobbles, sing a song
The world – no longer cold – begins to glow

I sing along!

His voice suggested languor, flat and set
But inside passion swirls like frenzied leaves
He made the tea and turned it to sat sang
While kindness kept on pouring from his sleeves

thank you Pei Wang!

Pei Wang is a Tea Artisan with a teahouse in Notting Hill. His life is tea.

茶

BEFORE IT GOES COLD

Actually, don't rush. Make a new pot. I'm about to.

Change the water, re-boil the kettle and decide which tea best says 'thank you' – because that's what these last few pages are all about.

Who Gets the Last Cup?

Oh crumbs, there's such a long line of cups waiting to be filled! Fortunately I made a massive pot…

The first must go to Heather Holden-Brown at hhb agency responding to a tepid approach for help and generously giving me her advice. Taking it led to Quiller Publishing. Every member of their charming team must enjoy the second cup, but the first sip belongs to Andrew Johnston for stepping outside his usual genre and making space for *Distinguished Leaves* in his list at the last minute. He achieved a minor miracle – a book proposal considered and agreed within a week.

The third cup must go to The Tea Box, Richmond. Here, I first tasted proper loose leaf tea and poetry together. Thank you, Mike and Jemma, for promoting 'poetea' at your Poetry Jams and for providing the inspiration behind the first tea poem, 'Moroccan Mint' – not to mention a hangover from numerous tastings of 'Irish Velvet'.

Of course, every contributor to this little volume: Nigel Havers, Tim D'Offay, Dechi Palmo, Henrietta Lovell, Jonathan Jones and Pei Wang deserve their own particular special brew. My pot overflows with gratitude.

Let me also pour a cup for each of the loose leaf tea establishments I've visited who (without exception) have welcomed both me and the opportunity to stock the book. The list is too long for these pages. The best thanks I can offer will depend on you, the reader. Discover these places and nosy out others for yourself. You'll find some of my favourites, at www.distinguishedleaves.com and I'm sure you'll enjoy your visits as much as I have mine.

That's it on the tea front. When it comes to poetry, let's raise two cups: to The Poetry Society and to Stephen Fry. If you're new to live poetry, discover the blend served up at the Society's 'Poetry Unplugged' every Tuesday, adroitly hosted by Niall O'Sullivan, and take it from there. To all my fellow poet friends, thank you, I am always learning from you.

And as for Stephen Fry? He's been my secret teacher. His genius in making 'the rules' fun (and understandable) is overshadowed by his celebrity status. But had it not been for his *The Ode Less Travelled* this volume would have been nothing more than a weak bag of 'tum-ti-tums'. Thank you. I doubt Quiller would have given me a second look without your unwitting help.

The penultimate cup must go to Peter and his team of beaming beauties at dIsH Café, Hampton Court, who (I reckon) serve the best *coffee* in London. Ironically, it was here that many of these poems were crafted post tea-tasting.

And finally, the final cup goes to two darling friends – my parents – who've had to share their home with a deranged tea-talking poet for far longer than first envisaged.

We have reached the dregs!

If I Was a Tea…

What a lovely thought! Of course I'd *like* The Darcy Jones Blend* to betray scents of the exquisite, gracious and poetic. Its taste would be distinctive, satisfying and sweet during consumption – enlivening the senses in every way…

TERROIR: The terroir unconsciously shapes us. The varietal I come from seems to thrive on daily exposure to silence, solitude and Pu-Erh tea. It also needs ground pulsating with creative initiatives. Companion plants tend to have artistic qualities. It provides shade for one individual at a time to enjoy its shelter. It dies in crowds.

After growing up writing poetry at school instead of doing maths, this tea-bush branched out from a secretarial career to voice coaching multi-millionaire businessmen for royal stockbrokers (Cazenove & Co). At this time its growth was confined to South Kensington's broom cupboard, 'The Hat Box'.

The Darcy Jones tea-bush had a slow developing literary habit, being blown by harsh winds and storms and being uprooted from London, to Wales, to Cornwall before returning to its native soil in South London. Various buds formed, including (in 1998) being commissioned to write the post-war biography of the SOE coding genius, Leo Marks OBE (and author of the famous poem-code, 'The Life That I Have').

The bush first produced a harvest in 2005 when *Simply*

* Since writing the book I now do have my own Tea Poet's Tisane! It has been created by Pei Wang and is a fragrant mix of Pu-Erh and rosebuds, that can be enjoyed as it is or with a little honey. See website for details.

花

This, a book of life affirming poetry, was published. By 2009, in West Cornwall, the bush was flowering abundantly but producing portrait miniatures rather than books from Lizzie Limner's Gallery, Marazion.

In 2010 the bush re-established itself up river from the historic home of tea – Twickenham, South London – where it is very happily maturing and growing hundreds of paper leaves, mainly of the poetic variety.

If you were a tea, what sort of tea would you be?

More?

Hundreds more teas and tisanes are begging to be celebrated in 'poetea' – from the curiously named Malawi Antlers, to hearty builders' tea. So the next volume is growing and it'll also include poems about some of my favourite tea haunts.

In the meantime, why not organise a 'poetea' event combining a tea-tasting and your own poems about tea? Of course, I'm always delighted to receive recital or invitations to perform. It's also satisfying to write 'non-tea poems' to commission for guests of honour or special events. Want to hear some live 'poetea'? There's a list of events on my website: www.teapoet.com or you can e-mail me at: poemsfortealovers@gmail.com. Let's talk poetry and tea via my blog at www.distinguishedleaves.com

Facebook isn't my bag so forgive me if I don't accept friend requests. I leave Twittering to Quiller!

Alphabetical List of Poems by Title

It All Boils Down to This…

'Tea's greatest gift is to put a cup of now in your hands.'
Anon

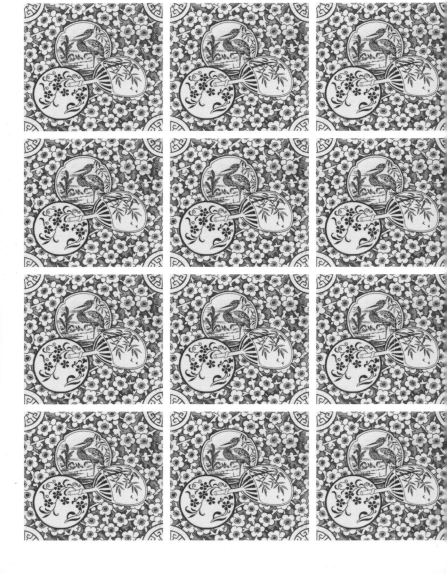